Practical
Pre-School

Planning for Learning through Colour

Rachel Sparks Linfield and Penny Coltman Illustrated by Cathy Hughes

Contents

Published by Step Forward Publishing Limited
The Coach House, Cross Road, Milverton, Leamington Spa CV32 5PB Tel: 01926 420046
© Step Forward Publishing Limited 2000
Planning for Learning through Colour ISBN: 1 902438 40 X

MAKING PLANS

WHY PLAN?

The purpose of planning is to make sure that all children enjoy a broad and balanced curriculum. All planning should be useful. Plans are working documents which you spend time preparing, but which should later repay your efforts. Try to be concise. This will help you in finding information quickly when you need it.

LONG-TERM PLANS

Preparing a long-term plan, which maps out the curriculum during a year or even two, will help you to ensure that you are providing a variety of activities and are meeting the statutory requirements of the *Curriculum Guidance for the Foundation Stage* (2000).

Your long-term plan need not be detailed. Divide the time period over which you are planning into fairly equal sections, such as half terms. Choose a topic for each section. Young children benefit from making links between the new ideas they encounter so as you select each topic, think about the time of year in which you plan to do it. A topic about minibeasts will not be very successful in November!

Although each topic will address all the learning areas, some could focus on a specific area. For example, a topic on Colour lends itself well to activities relating to creative areas and knowledge and understanding of the world. Another topic might particularly encourage the appreciation of stories. Try to make sure that you provide a variety of topics in your long-term plans.

Autumn 1	Colour
Autumn 2	Autumn/Christmas
Spring 1	Once upon a time
Spring 2	Changes
Summer 1	Toys
Summer 2	Out and about

MEDIUM-TERM PLANS

Medium-term plans will outline the contents of a topic in a little more detail. One way to start this process is by brainstorming on a large piece of paper. Work with your team writing down all the activities you can think of which are relevant to the topic. As you do this it may become clear that some activities go well together. Think about dividing them into themes. Colour, for example, has themes such as 'Black and white', 'Red', 'Mixing colours' and 'Rainbows'.

At this stage it is helpful to make a chart. Write the theme ideas down the side of the chart and put a different area of learning at the top of each column. Now you can insert your brainstormed ideas and quickly see where there are gaps. As you complete the chart take account of children's earlier experiences and provide opportunities for them to progress.

Refer back to the *Curriculum Guidance for the Foundation Stage* and check that you have addressed as many different aspects as you can. Once all your medium-term plans are complete make sure that there are no neglected areas.

DAY-TO-DAY PLANS

The plans you make for each day will outline aspects such as:

- resources needed;
- the way in which you might introduce activities;
- the organisation of adult help;
- size of the group;
- timing.

Identify the learning which each activity is intended to promote. Make a note of any assessments or observations that you are likely to carry out. On your plans make notes of which activities were particularly successful, or any changes you would make another time.

MAKING PLANS

A FINAL NOTE

Planning should be seen as flexible. Not all groups meet every day, and not all children attend every day. Any part of the plan can be used independently, stretched over a longer period or condensed to meet the needs of any group. This is particularly true of a topic such as Colour. Indeed some groups may wish to take on different colours during different parts of the year. Red, for example, is a wonderful colour to look at during autumn when leaves change whilst blue is often thought of as a cold, wintry colour. You will almost certainly adapt the activities as children respond to them in different ways and bring their own ideas, interests and enthusiasms. In addition, some children may be colour blind and need activities to be changed slightly to cater for their needs. The most common type of colour blindness is the inability to differentiate between red and green. The important thing is to ensure that the children are provided with a varied and enjoyable curriculum which meets their individual developing needs.

USING THE BOOK:

- Collect or prepare suggested resources as listed on page 21.

- Read the section which outlines links to the Early Learning Goals (pages 4 - 7) and explains the rationale for the topic of Colour.

- For each weekly theme two activities are described in detail as an example to help you in your planning and preparation. Key vocabulary, questions and learning opportunities are identified.

- The skills chart on page 23 will help you to see at a glance which aspects of children's development are being addressed as a focus each week.

- As children take part in the Colour topic activities, their learning will progress. 'Collecting evidence' on page 22 explains how you might monitor children's achievements.

- Find out on page 20 how the topic can be brought together in a grand finale involving parents, children and friends.

- There is additional material to support the working partnership of families and children in the form of a 'Home links' page, and a photocopiable 'Parent's page' found at the back of the book.

It is important to appreciate that the ideas presented in this book will only be a part of your planning. Many activities that will be taking place as routine in your group may not be mentioned. For example, it is assumed that sand, dough, water, puzzles, floor toys and large scale apparatus are part of the ongoing pre-school experience. Many groups will also be able to provide access to computers and other aspects of information and communication technology. Role play areas, stories, rhymes and singing, and group discussion times are similarly assumed to be happening each week although they may not be a focus for described activities.

USING THE EARLY LEARNING GOALS

Having decided on your topic and made your medium-term plans you can use the Early Learning Goals to highlight the key learning opportunities your activities will address. The Early Learning Goals are split into six areas: Personal, Social and Emotional Development, Communication, Language and Literacy, Mathematical Development, Knowledge and Understanding of the World, Physical Development and Creative Development. Do not expect each of your topics to cover every goal but your long-term plans should allow for each child to work towards all of the goals.

The following section highlights parts of the *Curriculum Guidance for the Foundation Stage* (2000) in point form to show what children are expected to be able to do in each area of learning by the time they enter Year 1. These points will be used throughout this book to show how activities for a topic on Colour link to these expectations. For example, Personal, Social and Emotional development point 8 is 'work as part of a group or class taking turns'. Activities suggested which provide the opportunity for children to do this will have the reference PS8. This will enable you to see which parts of the Early Learning Goals are covered in a given week and plan for areas to be revisited and developed.

In addition you can ensure that activities offer variety in the outcomes to be encountered. Often a similar activity may be carried out to achieve different outcomes. For example, during this topic children make symmetrical butterflies. They will be learning about shape and symmetry but they will also be discovering aspects of technology as they fold the paper, draw and cut out their design. It is important therefore that activities have clearly defined learning outcomes so that these may be emphasised during the activity and for recording purposes.

PERSONAL, SOCIAL AND EMOTIONAL DEVELOPMENT (PS)

This area of learning covers important aspects of development which affect the way children learn, behave and relate to others.

By the end of the Foundation Stage most children will:

PS1 continue to be interested, excited and motivated to learn

PS2 be confident to try new activities, initiate ideas and speak in a familiar group

PS3 maintain attention, concentrate, and sit quietly when appropriate

PS4 have a developing awareness of their own needs, views and feelings and be sensitive to the needs, views and feelings of others

PS5 have a developing respect for their own cultures and beliefs and those of other people

PS6 respond to significant experiences showing a range of feelings when appropriate

PS7 form good relationships with peers and adults

PS8 work as a part of a group or class taking turns and sharing fairly; understanding that there need to be agreed values and codes of behaviour for groups of people, including adults and children, to work harmoniously

PS9 understand what is right, what is wrong and why

PS10 dress and undress independently and manage their own personal hygiene

PS11 select and use activities and resources independently

PS12 consider the consequences of their words and actions for themselves and others

PS13 understand that people have different needs, views, cultures and beliefs which need to be treated with respect

PS14 understand that they can expect others to treat their needs, views, cultures and beliefs with respect

The topic of Colour offers many opportunities for children's personal, social and emotional development. Time spent discussing what colours mean and favourite colours will help children to show a range of feelings, to listen and to deal sensitively with others. By playing circle games children will learn to take turns and to understand the need for agreed codes of behaviour. Many of the areas outlined above, though, will be covered on an almost incidental basis as children carry out the activities described in this book for the other areas of learning. During undirected free choice times they will be developing independence (PS11) whilst any small group activity which involves working with an adult will help children to build effective relationships (PS7).

COMMUNICATION, LANGUAGE AND LITERACY (L)

The objectives set out in the *National literacy strategy: Framework for teaching* for the reception year are in line with these goals. By the end of the Foundation Stage, most children will be able to:

L1 enjoy listening to and using spoken and written language, and readily turn to it in their play and learning

L2 explore and experiment with sounds, words and texts

L3 listen with enjoyment and respond to stories, songs and other music, rhymes and poems and make up their own stories, songs, rhymes and poems

L4 use language to imagine and recreate roles and experiences

L5 use talk to organise, sequence and clarify thinking, ideas, feelings and events

L6 sustain attentive listening, responding to what they have heard by relevant comments, questions or actions

L7 interact with others, negotiating plans and activities and taking turns in conversation

L8 extend their vocabulary, exploring the meaning and sounds of new words

L9 retell narratives in the correct sequence, drawing on the language patterns of stories

L10 speak clearly and audibly with confidence and control and show awareness of the listener, for example by their use of conventions such as greetings, 'please' and 'thank you'

L11 hear and say initial and final sounds in words and short vowel sounds within words

L12 link sounds to letters, naming and sounding the letters of the alphabet

L13 read a range of familiar and common words and simple sentences independently

L14 show an understanding of the elements of stories such as main character, sequence of events, and openings and how information can be found in non-fiction texts to answer questions about where, who, why and how

L15 know that print carries meaning and, in English, is read from left to right and top to bottom

L16 attempt writing for various purposes, using features of different forms such as lists, stories and instructions

L17 write their own names, labels and captions, and begin to form sentences, sometimes using punctuation

L18 use their phonic knowledge to write simple regular words and make phonetically plausible attempts at more compex words

L19 use a pencil and hold it effectively to form recognisable letters, most of which are correctly formed

The activities suggested for the theme of Colour include several which are based on well-known, quality picture books and stories. They allow children to enjoy listening to the books and to respond in a variety of ways to what they hear, reinforcing and extending their vocabularies. Throughout the topic opportunities are described in which children are encouraged to explore the sounds of words, to use descriptive vocabulary and to see some of their ideas recorded in both pictures and words.

MATHEMATICAL DEVELOPMENT (M)

The key objectives in the *National numeracy strategy: Framework for teaching* for the reception year are in line with these goals. By the end of the Foundation Stage, most children will be able to:

M1 say and use number names in order in familiar contexts

M2 count reliably up to ten everyday objects;

M3 recognise numerals 1 to 9

M4 use language such as 'more' or 'less' to compare two numbers

M5 in practical activities and discussion begin to use the vocabulary involved in adding and subtracting

M6 find one more or one less than a number from one to ten

M7 begin to relate addition to combining two groups of objects and subtraction to 'taking away'

M8 talk about, recognise and recreate simple patterns

M9 use language such as 'circle' or 'bigger' to describe the shape and size of solids and flat shapes

M10 use everyday words to describe position

M11 use developing mathematical ideas and methods to solve practical problems

M12 use language such as 'greater', 'smaller', 'heavier' or 'lighter' to compare quantities

The theme of Colour provides a meaningful context for mathematical activities presented in a very visual way. A number of them allow children to sort and to create patterns based on colours. Children are given the opportunity to count coloured objects and to begin to develop language for addition and subtraction.

KNOWLEDGE AND UNDERSTANDING OF THE WORLD (K)

These goals provide a foundation for scientific, technological, historical and geographical learning.

By the end of the Foundation Stage most children will be able to:

K1 investigate objects and materials by using all of their senses as appropriate

K2 find out about and identify some features of, living things, objects and events they observe

K3 look closely at similarities, differences, patterns and change

K4 ask questions about why things happen and how things work

K5 build and construct with a wide range of objects, selecting appropriate resources and adapting their work where necessary

K6 select tools and techniques they need to shape, assemble and join the materials they are using

K7 find out about and identify the uses of everyday technology and use communication technology and programmable toys to support their learning

K8 find out about past and present events in their own lives, and in those of their families and other people they know

K9 observe, find out about and identify features in the place they live and the natural world

K10 begin to know about their own cultures and beliefs and those of other people

K11 find out about their environment and talk about those features they like and dislike

The topic of Colour offers many opportunities for children to experiment, to make observations and to ask questions. They can explore the effect of wind on blue streamers, the appearance of their environment as they look through pieces of coloured acetate and how black newspaper print appears when viewed through a magnifier. Children will be keen to look for similarities and change. By observing and describing apples and sunflowers they will begin to be aware of features of fruits and flowers.

PHYSICAL DEVELOPMENT (PD)

By the end of the Foundation Stage most children will be able to:

PD1 move with confidence, imagination and in safety

PD2 move with control and co-ordination

PD3 show awareness of space, of themselves and of others

PD4 recognise the importance of keeping healthy and those things which contribute to this

PD5 recognise the changes that happen to their bodies when they are active

PD6 use a range of small and large equipment

PD7 travel around, under, over and through balancing and climbing equipment

PD8 handle tools, objects, construction and malleable materials safely with increasing control.

Activities such as playing with coloured playdough or peg boards will offer experience of PD8. Through pretending to be animals getting on and off Noah's ark and chasing an imaginary balloon children will have the opportunity to develop PD1, 2 and 3. As children play more active games, such as traffic lights, they will become more aware of how their bodies change.

CREATIVE DEVELOPMENT (C)

By the end of the Foundation Stage most children will be able to:

C1 explore colour, texture, shape, form and space in two or three dimensions

C2 recognise and explore how sounds can be changed, sing simple songs from memory, recognise repeated sounds and sound patterns and match movements to music

C3 respond in a variety of ways to what they see, hear, smell, touch and feel

C4 use their imagination in art and design, music, dance, imaginative and role play and stories

C5 express and communicate their ideas, thoughts and feelings by using a widening range of materials, suitable tools, imaginative and role play, movement, designing and making, and a variety of songs and musical instruments

During this topic children will experience working with a variety of materials as they make models, for example of Noah's ark. They will have ample opportunity to develop their skills of painting and colour mixing and so work towards C1 and 4. A number of songs which have colours or rainbows in them have been suggested which could also have actions and percussion added, so allowing children to use their imagination in music. Throughout all the activities children are encouraged to talk about what they see and feel as they communicate their ideas in painting, collage work and role play.

Week 1

BLACK AND WHITE

PERSONAL, SOCIAL AND EMOTIONAL DEVELOPMENT

- To introduce both the overall topic and the week's theme go on a colour detecting walk. Before leaving, talk about the importance of listening to instructions and staying together. Help children to notice that there is variation in the shades and tones of a particular colour. Explain that this week they will be focusing on black and white. How many things can they find that are just black or white? (PS1, 6, 8)

- Show children a piece of paper with a small spot of ink on it. Ask them what they see. Most are likely to tell you that they see a spot and not mention the rest of the paper. Talk about the importance of not only noticing when things are wrong. (PS3, 4)

- Invite a road safety officer (contact through your local authority) to talk about how to cross roads safely and the importance of using zebra crossings where available. (PS3, 7, 9, 12)

COMMUNICATION, LANGUAGE AND LITERACY

- Begin a big book colour dictionary (see activity opposite). (L11, 13)

- Read *Elmer and Wilbur* by David McKee. Talk about the colours on Elmer and Wilbur. Does Elmer have any black on him? How are the two elephants similar? How are they different? (L6, 10)

- Talk about opposites and the fact that black is the opposite of white. Read *Opposites* by Nick Butterworth and Mick Inkpen (Hodder Children's Books). Play a game in which children are picked to do the opposite of what they are told. (L3, 6, 8)

MATHEMATICAL DEVELOPMENT

- Put out a selection of 2-D and 3-D shapes and shadows cut out from black sugar paper. Ask children to match the shapes to their shadows. Encourage them to use the correct names for the shapes. (M9)

- Use bought or home-made blocks to print a repeating pattern using white paint on black sugar paper. Can the children continue the pattern? (M8)

- Play games using black and white dice and dominoes. Encourage children to count the spots as they play. (M2, 5)

KNOWLEDGE AND UNDERSTANDING OF THE WORLD

- Read *Winnie the Witch* by Korky Paul and Valerie Thomas (Oxford University Press). Discuss why Winnie could not see her cat in the black house. Use wax crayons or chalks to draw a black cat 'hiding' in a black room. (K1, 3)

- Discuss why white is a good colour to wear at night. Lay pieces of paper of different colours on a sheet of black paper. Talk about evenings when it is dark. Investigate which colours can be seen from a distance on the black background. (K1, 3)

- Look at some pictures of animals which are black and white such as pandas and zebras. On black paper, use only white paint to make pictures of zebras, polar bears and pandas (see activity opposite). (K9)

- Encourage children to use magnifiers as they examine black and white newspaper pictures. Draw attention to the many tiny dots which are closely packed to make the picture. (K2)

PHYSICAL DEVELOPMENT

- Weave black and white strips of paper to make mats. (PD6, 8)

- Use white modelling dough made from cornflour to make snow animals. Display against a black background. (PD6, 8)

- Use white playground chalk to draw lines on the ground for children to move along in a variety of ways. Encourage children to listen to instructions telling them how and when to move, and to stay on the lines. (PD1, 2)

CREATIVE DEVELOPMENT

- Do a collage using newsprint on either black or white paper. Encourage children to compare the appearance of the pictures on the white and the black backgrounds. (C1, 4)

- Show children how white can be added to black paint a little at a time to make a series of greys. How many greys can the group make? (C1)

- Make spinners from stiff white card circles with a short pencil through the centre. Show children how to draw patterns such as spirals, parallel straight lines or zig zag lines with a black pen and spin the spinners. What happens to their patterns? How do the patterns make them feel? (C1, 5)

ACTIVITY: PAINTING ANIMALS ON BLACK PAPER

Learning opportunity: Discussing why zebras and pandas have distinct markings. Painting pictures of animals using only white paint on black paper.

Early Learning Goal: Knowledge and Understanding of the World. Children will be able to find out about and identify features in the natural world.

Resources: White ready-mixed paint; a selection of thin and thicker brushes; white chalk; A4 and A3 sized pieces of black paper; pictures of pandas, zebras and polar bears.

Key vocabulary: Black, white, zebra, panda, polar bear.

Organisation: Small group.

WHAT TO DO:

Show the group the pictures of the animals. Check that children know what they are. Has anyone ever seen one? Look closely at the markings on the zebras and the pandas. Tell the children that all zebras have different markings - no two are the same. Explain that the panda's black and white face warns other animals to stay away. On a piece of black paper paint a few stripes like a zebra's and ask children what they think you have painted. Invite the children to paint either a polar bear, a panda or a zebra using only white paint - explain that the black parts of the animals will not need to be painted. Some may wish to draw their animal with chalk before painting, others may want to try painting stripes and other white patterns on black paper before having a go at an animal.

ACTIVITY: COLOUR DICTIONARY

Learning opportunity: Co-operating to make a colour dictionary and reading the names of colours.

Early Learning Goal: Communication, Language and Literacy. Children will be able to hear and say initial sounds in words. They will read a range of familiar words.

Resources: A big book with A1 sized pages made from pieces of black, white, red, yellow, blue, green, orange and purple card. The name of the colour should be written clearly at the top of each page. You also need a simple, well illustrated dictionary and a book about colours - for example *Maisy's Colours* by Lucy Cousins (Walker Books); a basket containing pictures of objects; and scraps of papers in a variety of colours but predominantly black and white.

Key vocabulary: Dictionary, book, black, white, red, yellow, blue, green, orange, purple.

Organisation: Whole group.

WHAT TO DO:

Show the group the dictionary. Tell the children it is a dictionary and ask them if they know what it is used for. Ask them to suggest words which they might look up in the dictionary. What sounds do they begin with? Look up the words. Show the children the colour dictionary. Help them to read the words written on each page. Explain to the group that the dictionary will contain pictures of things that are a particular colour, scraps which are the colour and words. Today they are going to begin the black and white pages. Ask a child to come and select a black picture from the basket. What is it? Stick the picture on the black page and scribe with a white crayon what the object is. Invite other children to select black or white pictures and scraps. Ask the children to bring from home scraps and pictures for the colour dictionary.

DISPLAY

Mount the grey paintings together to form a stunning large patchwork. Edge the patchwork with a border of white paper next to a strip of black.

Cut around the children's black and white animals and mount them on white paper. Cover a board with black backing paper and stick on white silhouettes of trees, grass and bamboo. Arrange the animals on the scene.

Week 2

RED

PERSONAL, SOCIAL AND EMOTIONAL DEVELOPMENT

- During circle time talk about red things the group likes. Pass a red object around and encourage the children to speak only when they hold the red object. (PS2, 3, 4, 8)

- Talk about the idea of going red. Sometimes this can be when we feel embarrassed, or it may be when we feel angry, hot, upset or after exercise. Read the story of *Where the Wild Things Are* by Maurice Sendak (Red Fox). Max is sent to his room because he has misbehaved and his mother is angry. (PS2, 3, 4, 6, 8)

- Read the story of *Little Red Riding Hood* by Jonathan Langley (Picture Lions). This retelling of an old tale has a number of messages which can be discussed. (PS 2, 3, 4, 8, 12)

COMMUNICATION, LANGUAGE AND LITERACY

- On a large sheet of paper write the word red. Draw attention to the initial sound r. Encourage children to think of the names of objects or even people beginning with the same sound. Put the word red in front of each of these words to produce a variety of sensible and nonsensical phrases. (L2, 11)

- Write a large group poem for the title *What is red?* Each child should use the words 'Red is' to start their line. Either scribe the suggestions or encourage children to overwrite in red crayon, underwrite or write to make a class poem display. (L6, 16, 18, 19)

- Begin to make a colour book box. Put in it books which have red as a central theme such as *Ready for Red* by Candace Whitman (Abbeville Kids). Allow children to choose a different story from the box each day. Add to the box as the colour theme weeks progress. (L3, 14)

MATHEMATICAL DEVELOPMENT

- Play the 'In the red box' game (see activity opposite). (M2, 5, 6)

- Sing the following number rhyme to the tune of 'Ten green bottles':

  Five red poppies on a sunny day,
  (*Hold up five fingers*)

  Five red poppies on a sunny day,

  And if one red poppy is picked along the way,
  (*Fold down one finger*)

  There'll be four red poppies on a sunny day.

  Encourage the children to count the remaining poppies between each verse to reinforce the forward counting sequence. (M5, 6)

- Encourage each child to make their own picture to illustrate the song, making red flowers from paper circles. Introduce the words circle and round. (M9)

KNOWLEDGE AND UNDERSTANDING OF THE WORLD

- Red is often used as a warning. Look at pictures of road signs which have red borders and discuss their meanings. Give the children prepared paper shapes mounted with a wide red border on which they can design their own warning signs for their room. (K2, 9)

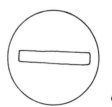  

- Go outside and use pieces of red acetate to see what the world would be like if it was red. (K3)

- Look at a shiny red apple. Use chalks or pastels to make a picture of the apple. Show children how to use small pieces of cotton wool or sponge to smudge the colours. Cut the apple and taste it. Ask children to describe what it tastes like. (K1)

PHYSICAL DEVELOPMENT

- Play the traffic lights game (see activity opposite). (PD1, 2, 3)

- Use red playdough on the modelling table. (PD6, 8)

- After an energetic movement session, encourage the children to notice that some of their faces will have become redder. (PD5)

CREATIVE DEVELOPMENT

- Provide children with an outline of an apple drawn on A4 white card, glue and scraps of mainly red tissue paper. Show children how to cover the apple with pieces of overlapping tissue. Varnish the apple with watered down PVA glue. From black A4 paper or card cut apple shaped windows slightly smaller than the tissue apples. Put the frames on and stick the pictures up in a window where the sunlight can shine through. (C1, 3)

- Explain to children that when white is added to a colour it makes a tone. Ask children to see how many different tones they can make by adding white to red, using the colours to paint bands down a piece of paper. Once they are dry, use them as the backgrounds for red sunset pictures, sticking black silhouettes onto them, or blow painting black tree shapes. (C1, 3, 5)

ACTIVITY: IN THE RED BOX GAME

Learning opportunity: Counting to five and beginning to visualise the number bonds to five.

Early Learning Goal: Mathematical Development. Children will be able to count reliably up to ten everyday objects. They will begin to use vocabulary involved in adding and subtracting.

Resources: A red box or bucket with a lid containing five identical red objects; five more identical red objects.

Key vocabulary: Numbers one to five. How many?

Organisation: Whole group.

WHAT TO DO:

Show the children the red box. Shake it. What do they think is in the box? How many do they think are in it? Take the lid off and ask children to help you count the objects. Establish that there are five. Put two objects in the box and put the lid on. Ask children how many are in the box. Put two more in and again ask how many are in. Take one out. How many are there now? Continue to put in and take out objects, encouraging children to say how many there are. Once children are confident with this activity, ask them to shut their eyes and to imagine the box. Tell them you have put two red cubes in their box. Can they see them? You put in

one more. How many are in the box? In future sessions encourage children to think more quickly and gradually introduce numbers to ten.

ACTIVITY: TRAFFIC LIGHTS GAME

Learning opportunity: Moving with confidence and co-ordination according to instructions indicated by traffic light colours. Listening carefully to instructions.

Early Learning Goal: Physical Development. Children will be able to move safely with confidence, co-ordination and control. They will show awareness of space, themselves and others.

Resources: Large space where children can run and also sit comfortably on the floor.

Key vocabulary: Red, yellow, green, go, start, stop, walk, sit, jump.

Organisation: Whole group.

WHAT TO DO:

Ask children whether they have ever seen a traffic light. What does the red light mean? What does the green one let traffic do? Explain that the group is going to play a game called traffic lights. Ask a child to demonstrate. Explain that when you call 'green' they can walk. When you say 'red' they must stop. Ask the child to follow your instructions. Repeat this with the whole group, varying the way you say the colours to encourage children to listen to what you say and not simply how you say it. Once children are confident with red and green, introduce yellow as the instruction for jumping. In further sessions the game can be extended to include blue to mean 'sit down'.

DISPLAY

Cover a noticeboard with the tones paintings. On a table in front of this place a box containing scraps of a variety of pink papers. Encourage children to match the papers to the tones.

Arrange the apple pictures near the tissue paper apples on the windows. Write words suggested by the children which describe the apple's taste and appearance. Stick these near the apples.

Week 3

YELLOW

PERSONAL, SOCIAL AND EMOTIONAL DEVELOPMENT

- Many people who help us wear yellow clothes to help them to be seen: fire fighters, ambulance paramedics, road crossing attendants. Equip the dressing-up box with suitable yellow clothes - fireman's hat, yellow tabards - to encourage role play and independent dressing. (PS8, 10, 11)

- Many children will associate the colour yellow with sunshine. Use this opportunity to talk about the importance of the sun in our lives providing warmth and light. (PS2, 3)

COMMUNICATION, LANGUAGE AND LITERACY

- Look at the picture book *Sunshine* by Jan Ormerod. The pictures show the sequence of events as a child wakes in the morning and gets ready for school. Encourage the children to talk about the sequence, predicting what might happen next and describing the pictures. (L1, 4, 5, 6, 9)

- Play 'I went shopping......' but only allow yellow purchases! Help the children by reminding them about yellow foods: dairy products, fruits, juices and pastas. Invite one child to start the game with 'I went shopping and bought a ......' Following children must remember the items already on the list before adding their own. (L1, 6)

- Make a collection of simple pictures of familiar yellow objects. Encourage children to take turns in picking one of the pictures out of a box. They describe it to the rest of the group who try to guess what it is. (L1, 3, 5)

MATHEMATICAL DEVELOPMENT

- Show children how to make butterflies from coloured paper by folding paper in half, drawing a body and two wings and cutting it out. Talk about the fact that it is symmetrical and use mirrors to show that one half is the mirror image of the other. (M9)

- Provide sticky yellow dots. Encourage the children to stick one, two or three dots on each wing of their butterfly. Use this as an introduction to doubles. (M1, 2, 4)

- Use yellow fruits, pasta or pulses for weighing activities. How many shells will balance the banana? How much pasta will balance the car? Which is heavier - the banana or the car? (M12)

- Use pasta or yellow lentils to fill containers and packets in role play shopping or cooking. (M11)

KNOWLEDGE AND UNDERSTANDING OF THE WORLD

- Discuss the fact that insects like yellow flowers. Look through seed catalogues to find flowers which attract insects. Make collage flowers from a variety of materials such as wood shavings dyed with food colouring, yellow cellophane, yellow tissues and crepe, pasta, drinking straws, textiles and so on. (K2)

- Make a collection of yellow flowers such as daffodils or buttercups. Talk about the names for parts of the plant such as stalk, leaf and petal. Encourage the children to make observational drawings which show the correct number of petals. (K2, 3)

- Make yellow chicks from two yellow cotton wool balls glued together. Fold orange paper diamonds to make beaks, add tiny black paper eyes and glue the chick onto pre-cut black paper feet. (K5, 6)

PHYSICAL DEVELOPMENT

- Cover a table with black bin-liner plastic and allow free play with bright yellow finger paint. Prints of the results can be made using black paper. (PD2, 8)

- Invite children to mime the sequence of events as you tell the story of waking on a sunny day, dressing and leaving home to go to the shops or outside to play (see activity opposite). (PD1)

- Allow free play with yellow bean bags, balls and hoops. (PD6)

CREATIVE DEVELOPMENT

- Read *Billy's Sunflower* by Nicola Moon (Little Hippo). Make pot pourri sunflowers (see activity opposite). (C1)

- Use pastels and chalks to make drawings of sunflowers on black paper. (C1)

- Use tuned and untuned percussion to provide sound effects for the story of waking on a sunny day. Tape record the story with sound effects and ask children to listen. How useful were the sounds? What other sounds could be added to improve the tale? (C4)

ACTIVITY: POT POURRI SUNFLOWERS

Learning opportunity: Making models of sunflowers and describing the scent of pot pourri.

Early Learning Goal: Creative Development. Children will be able to explore colour, shape and form in two or three dimensions. They will respond to what they smell.

Resources: A real or artificial sunflower; glue; a hole punch; black felt pens; *Billy's Sunflower* by Nicola Moon (Little Hippo); for each child a small plastic plant pot; a marble sized piece of Plasticine; a green wooden garden cane about 30 cm long; two yellow card circles about 7 cm in diameter; orange petals to glue around the circle; two green card or stiff paper leaves; a pot full of pot pourri; two paper-clips; sticky tape; cling-film to cover the pot; an A3 sheet of plain newsprint.

Key vocabulary: Sunflower, leaf, petal, stalk, seed.

Organisation: Small group.

WHAT TO DO:

Read *Billy's Sunflower* by Nicola Moon. Have any of the children ever grown a sunflower? Show the group the sunflowers. Talk about the different parts of the flower. Explain that they are going to make a sunflower as a present for someone in their family. (They make ideal presents for Mothers' Day.) Show the children how to make black dots all over their card circle like the sunflower seeds, stick petals around its edge and tape a cane to the centre of the circle. Finally the children should glue a second circle to the first to hide the cane and tape, and paper clip the circles together. Once dry the clips can be removed.

At a second session show children how to punch holes in two leaves and thread them on to the cane stalk. Ask the children to smell the pot pourris and to describe their scents. Ask them to select one for their flower. Stand the flower in a pot with the aid of a lump of Plasticine.

Fill the pot with pot pourri and cover the pot with cling-film, securing it firmly with pretty tape or a ribbon. Decorate the plain sheet of paper for wrapping paper for when the flowers are finally taken home.

ACTIVITY: WAKEY! WAKEY!

Learning opportunity: Miming imaginatively to spoken instructions.

Early Learning Goal: Physical Development. Children will be able to move with confidence, imagination and control.

Resources: Large space.

Key vocabulary: Stretch, waking, sensory words, names for articles of clothing.

Organisation: Whole group.

WHAT TO DO:

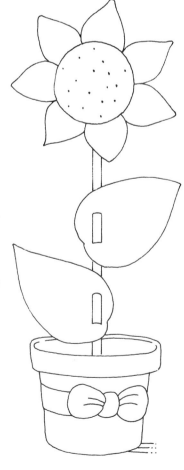

You may decide to introduce the activity by re-visiting *Sunshine* by Jan Ormerod.

Tell the story of a child waking from a deep sleep on a warm summer's day. As you lead the children through the actions of waking, getting out of bed, washing, dressing, breakfast, and so on, try to encourage children to think about sensory experiences: sounds, sights, feelings. Talk about the pushes and pulls as clothes are taken off and put on. Can children show through their miming that the shoes are hard to put on? How is putting on a cardigan different from pulling on a T-shirt? Talk about the sounds of breakfast cooking and the smell of toast or the taste of the cereal as children carry out the appropriate actions.

DISPLAY

Put up a picture of sunflowers such as a poster of the ones painted by Van Gogh alongside the children's pastel drawings. Arrange the children's sunflowers in plant pots on a table in front.

Week 4

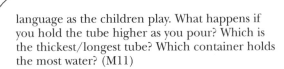

BLUE

PERSONAL, SOCIAL AND EMOTIONAL DEVELOPMENT

• During circle time take turns to play 'I spy something that is blue and ...'(PS8)

• Explain to the children what people mean when they say they 'feel blue'. Ask children to say what makes them 'feel blue' and what they could do to help people to be happier. (PS4)

COMMUNICATION, LANGUAGE AND LITERACY

• Read *The Blue Balloon* by Mick Inkpen(Hodder Children's Books). Ask children to retell the story from the pictures.(L6, 9)

• Ask children where they would like to travel on a blue balloon. Help children to record their ideas in words and pictures on balloons cut from blue card. Hang them up where they are free to blow in draughts and at heights where children can 'read' them. (L3, 13, 16, 18, 19)

• Put out a variety of blue writing materials to encourage emergent writing and pattern making. Provide blue paper of different thicknesses and shades, carbon paper, felt pens of different thicknesses, wax and pencil crayons. (L16, 19)

MATHEMATICAL DEVELOPMENT

• Make a large blue paper pond. Prepare ten cut-out paper fish and encourage the children to count them, moving those counted to a different part of the pond. Now remove some of the fish. Encourage the children to guess how many they think there are remaining in the pond, and to check their estimates by counting. (M1, 2)

• Colour the water in the water tray using blue food colouring. Provide plenty of transparent water toys, including tubing, plastic bottles, cups and funnels. Encourage the use of a variety of mathematical

language as the children play. What happens if you hold the tube higher as you pour? Which is the thickest/longest tube? Which container holds the most water? (M11)

• Prepare a basket of blue sticky paper shapes such as rectangles (including squares), circles, triangles and stars in a variety of sizes. Discuss the names of the shapes and their properties. Ask children to use the shapes to make a picture. At the end ask them to describe their pictures and to explain which shapes they have used. (M9)

KNOWLEDGE AND UNDERSTANDING OF THE WORLD

• Use blue liquid paint and washing-up liquid to make bubble prints (see activity opposite). (K1)

• Make paper streamers from different shades of blue crepe paper. Go outside to play with them on a windy day or enjoy running along watching the twirling shapes and patterns. (K3)

PHYSICAL DEVELOPMENT

• Use blue playdough on the modelling table. (PD8)

• Prepare blue card fish shapes. Punch holes around the edge and provide a range of blue wools and threads which can be laced. (PD6)

• Remind the children of the story of the blue balloon. Encourage them to move as balloons as you tell a story - starting small, being inflated, bobbing on the end of a string, blowing freely in the wind and finally deflating or even going pop!(PD1)

CREATIVE DEVELOPMENT

• On A3 or A4 pieces of paper show children how to paint a stripe of blue paint in the centre and then add black a little at a time to paint strips of blue tones in the lower half of the picture. Repeat this with white and blue paint for the other half. When dry these make attractive

Planning for Learning through Colour **Practical Pre-School**

watery backgrounds on which children can place cut-outs of assorted sea creatures, real shells or pasta shells sprayed with silver and gold paint.(C 1)

- Make a group collage of a peacock (see activity below). (C1)

- Sing a variety of traditional songs and rhymes associated with the word blue: 'Little Boy Blue', 'Lavender's Blue', 'In and Out the Dusky Bluebells'. (C5)

ACTIVITY: BUBBLE PRINTS

Learning opportunity: Making a print.

Early Learning Goal: Knowledge and Understanding of the World. Children will be able to investigate objects and materials by using all of their senses as appropriate.

Resources: Blue ready-mixed paint; washing-up liquid; one drinking straw per child; blotting paper circles or filter papers (named using a pencil); empty yogurt pots (large) or margarine tubs; table covering.

Key vocabulary: Blow, mix, bubbles, blue, print.

Organisation: Small group.

WHAT TO DO:

Half fill each container with blue ready-mixed paint which has been slightly watered down. Add a tablespoon of washing-up liquid to each pot.

Give each child their own drinking straw. Show how to keep the open end of the straw beneath the surface of the paint whilst blowing gently but steadily. Once the surface is covered with a thick layer of bubbles, lay a circle of blotting or filter paper carefully onto it. Explain that the paper should be lifted away again without moving it from side to side as this would spoil the print. Dry and display. If the prints are laminated they can make effective coasters for gifts on special occasions such as Mothers' Day!

ACTIVITY: COLLAGE PEACOCK

Learning opportunity: Making a collaborative collage.

Early Learning Goal: Creative Development. Children will be able to explore colour, texture, shape, form and space in two or three dimensions.

Resources: Peacock feathers or a picture of a peacock displaying its tail; pre-cut feather shapes in shades of blue card; shiny scraps such as sequins, ribbons, metallic papers, foils, and textiles; glue; scissors; card cut-out of peacock's body (front view); blue and green finger paints.

Key vocabulary: Sparkly, blue, shiny, feather, peacock, bird, beautiful.

Organisation: Small group.

WHAT TO DO:

Show the children a peacock feather or a photograph of a peacock with its tail on full display. Explain to the children that they are going to work together to make a big picture of a peacock with beautiful feathers like this. Start by inviting the children to decorate the cut-out of the peacock's body with finger paint. This will produce a feathered effect. Put this aside to dry.

Now present each child with a cut-out feather shape. Explain that they are going to decorate the feather as richly as they like using the sparkly and shiny materials. Encourage them to admire their feathers from a distance to see how attractive they look.

Assemble all the finished feathers in a fan shape on a display board and mount the body shape in front of them.

DISPLAY

Put the group's peacock on a large noticeboard. If possible, place a real peacock's feather nearby together with bird books depicting peacocks.

Put up the shape pictures. In a basket nearby place examples of the shapes used. Invite children to take turns to select a shape and to spot where it has been used.

Week 5
MIXING COLOURS

PERSONAL, SOCIAL AND EMOTIONAL DEVELOPMENT

- Play the 'Changing colours game' (see activity opposite). (PS8)

- Read *Elmer and the Lost Teddy* by David McKee (Andersen Press). Ask children to talk about a toy that is special to them and to say why. (PS2, 3, 4)

COMMUNICATION LANGUAGE AND LITERACY

- Prepare cards of several different colours and distribute them. As you tell a story, children listen for 'their' colour, holding up their card whenever it is mentioned. (L1, 3)

- Read *The Mixed-Up Chameleon* by Eric Carle (Picture Puffins). Begin a collection of colourful animal phrases for animals in the book. (L3, 6)

- Read *Picasso the Green Tree Frog* by Amanda Graham (Era), a story about a frog who falls in a jar of jelly beans, becomes multi-coloured and then has difficulties turning back into a green tree frog. Ask the children to invent ways for the frog to become totally green. (L1, 4)

MATHEMATICAL DEVELOPMENT

- Fill a basket with coloured counters or 'compare bears'. Ask children in turn to take a handful, to estimate how many they have and to count to see how near they were. (M2)

- Sort coloured counters into sets. Which set is the largest? Which is the smallest? How many more green counters are there than red? How many blue and yellow counters are there all together? (M2, 4, 5)

- Use beads/coloured macaroni tubes and thread to make necklaces of repeating patterns (see activity opposite). (M8)

KNOWLEDGE AND UNDERSTANDING OF THE WORLD

- Investigate what happens when water is sprayed onto white tissue paper and food colouring is dropped onto the tissue. (K1, 3, 4)

- Use colour paddles or coloured acetates to investigate what we see when we look through two different colours at the same time. (K1, 9)

- Make sunlight catchers by cutting a rectangle from four sides of a small box and sticking red, blue, yellow and one other coloured piece of acetate in the holes. Hang the boxes in a sunny window and encourage children to observe what happens as they catch the light. (K5, 9)

PHYSICAL DEVELOPMENT

- Allow free play with peg boards and multi-coloured pegs. (PD6)

- Practise throwing and catching with multi-coloured balls and bean bags. (PD6)

- Play aiming games in which a particular coloured bean bag is thrown into a particular coloured hoop or bucket. (PD6)

CREATIVE DEVELOPMENT

- Provide each child with a pre-drawn umbrella with six segments and a red, yellow and blue wax crayon. Ask children to colour three segments with the crayons and then show how green, purple and orange can be made by using two colours together. (C1)

- Use overlapping tissue papers to make colourful collages of mixed-up chameleons. (C1, 4, 5)

- Show children how to mix red, yellow and blue powder paints to make a wide range of colours. If brushes are dipped in water, dabbed on sponge and then placed in the powder paint a small amount of a good consistency will be collected for mixing on a plate or palette. Painting on black paper will encourage children to make rich colours. (C1, 4)

ACTIVITY: THE CHANGING COLOURS GAME

Learning opportunity: Playing a collaborative game.

Early Learning Goal: Personal, Social and Emotional Development. Children will work as part of a class, taking turns......

Resources: Postcard sized pieces of card in red, blue, yellow, white (there should be enough for each child to have one piece).

Key vocabulary: Red, blue, yellow, white.

Organisation: Whole group seated on chairs in a circle.

WHAT TO DO:

Remind children of the routines for circle time, such as only one person speaks at once and that we look at the person who is speaking. Hand out the pieces of card. Ask children in turn to say the name of their colour. Explain that they are going to play the changing colours game. Ask all the 'red children' to stand up. Explain that whenever you say the word 'red' they must change places quickly and quietly with someone else who is standing up. Ask the red group to demonstrate and praise those who did as you asked. Repeat this with the other three groups. Begin a story about painting a picture, encouraging children to change places whenever their colour is mentioned. (On future occasions the game can also include colours which are made with a combination of others - on 'green' the 'blue' and 'yellow' children would move or on 'pink' the 'white' and the 'red' groups would change places.)

Finish the session with each child saying why they like or dislike the colour they are holding.

ACTIVITY: MACARONI NECKLACES

Learning opportunity: Making necklaces which have repeating patterns.

Early Learning Goal: Mathematical Development. Children will be able to talk about, recognise and recreate simple patterns.

Resources: Macaroni tubes which have been coloured with food colouring*; thread; scissors; two macaroni tube necklaces with simple repeating patterns (red, blue, red, blue); small plastic tubs or coffee jar lids for holding the tubes.

Key vocabulary: Repeating pattern, names of colours, tube.

Organisation: Whole group introduction, small group for necklace making.

WHAT TO DO:

Introduction: Sit in a circle. Show children the macaroni tube necklaces and explain that everyone will be able to make one. Which necklace does the group like best? Why? Pick up the one the group prefers. Ask children to say the colour as you point to tubes in turn. Take a piece of thread and put a tube on it. Ask the group what you would need to put on next if you were to make another necklace just the same. Invite children to come and select tubes to continue the pattern. Show children the range of coloured tubes from which they will be able to pick up to three colours to use.

Necklace making: As a group, lay out a repeating pattern of tubes allowing each child to have a turn. Ask each child which colours they would like to use for their own necklace and give them the tubes in small tubs. Ask the children to show you the pattern they would like to do. Once children are happy with the idea of a repeating pattern let them begin to make their necklaces. As the children work, encourage them to say the names of the colours they are using to reinforce the repeating nature of the pattern.

* Dilute the food colouring to make about half a cupful of a strong solution. Mix this with the macaroni by shaking in a sealed polythene bag. Drain and blot with kitchen roll before spreading the macaroni evenly on a sheet of greaseproof paper on a large baking sheet. Dry very slowly in a gentle oven.

DISPLAY

Display the necklaces on a board covered with black sugar paper. In front place a basket containing the left-over macaroni tubes and thread for children to use during undirected times.

On a second board display the chameleon collages along with the book and also a selection of other picture books by Eric Carle such as *The Very Hungry Caterpillar*.

Week 6

RAINBOWS

PERSONAL, SOCIAL AND EMOTIONAL DEVELOPMENT

- Read *Noah's Ark* by Lucy Cousins (Walker Books). Discuss the fact that every living creature was important and all animals were taken on to the ark. (PS2, 3)

- Read *The Rainbow Fish* by Marcus Pfister (North-South Books) to introduce a discussion about the need to share. (PS2, 4, 9)

- Introduce the idea of a rainbow party and talk about the preparations that will need to take place. (PS1, 8)

COMMUNICATION, LANGUAGE AND LITERACY

- Read *Balloon* by Jez Alborough (Collins). This book about a rainbow coloured balloon uses the word 'it' repeatedly. Re-read the book and ask children to raise a hand each time the word 'it' is read. Begin a group collection of words which rhyme with 'it'. Provide children with cards on which the letters 'it' are printed. Either ask children to write a letter in front or scribe the letter to make the new word and ask them to illustrate it. (L3, 6, 18, 19)

- Make a pelmanism/memory type game in which words for colours are paired with coloured pieces of card. (L13)

- Provide each child with a rainbow book made from A5 sized pieces of paper, one for each colour in the rainbow. Show them the group's colour dictionary and ask them to make their own books of their favourite things for each colour. Each page could contain a picture and the word. (L16, 19)

MATHEMATICAL DEVELOPMENT

- The animals went into the ark in pairs. Provide socks cut from coloured paper for children to sort into pairs. Count the socks and the pairs. (M1, 2)

- Stick coloured dots on a dice and provide each child with a drawing of a rainbow with six sections. Children colour the rainbow according to the colour they throw. The winner is the child who uses the most colours. (M2, 8)

- Repeat the rainbow colouring game with a numbered dice. This time each number corresponds to a different colour. (M3)

KNOWLEDGE AND UNDERSTANDING OF THE WORLD

- Show children how rainbows can be made with a prism or clear plastic beaker of water which catches the sunlight on a windowsill. (K1, 2, 4)

- Make a chromatography rainbow name (see activity opposite). (K1, 3)

- Make rainbow biscuits for the rainbow party. (K1, 3, 4)

PHYSICAL DEVELOPMENT

- Use the story of Noah's ark for miming animal movements (see activity opposite). (PD1)

- On large apparatus pretend to be climbing, balancing and swinging animals. (PD1, 3, 7)

- Give children coloured streamers made from crepe paper or ribbon. Show them how to make swirling movements. Do a follow-my-leader rainbow dance encouraging children to watch carefully and to move exactly as you do. (PD2)

CREATIVE DEVELOPMENT

- Paint pictures of pairs of animals and a large rainbow for a whole group frieze of Noah's ark. (C1, 4)

- Make arks from boxes and paint them in rainbow colours. (C5)
- Sing 'Mr Noah Built an Ark' (in *Junior Praise*, Marshall Pickering) and 'Sing a Rainbow' (in *Apusskido Songs for Children*, A & C Black). Once children are familiar with the tunes and words, actions and percussion can be added. (C4)

ACTIVITY: RAINBOW NAMES

Learning opportunity: Observing changes to ink as blotting paper is dipped in water.

Early Learning Goal: Knowledge and Understanding of the World. Children will be able to look closely at.....differences and change.

Resources: Postcard sized pieces of blotting paper with children's names written at the top in pencil; black washable felt pens; large shallow tray of water to a depth of about 1 cm; waterproof tablecloth; a prepared rainbow name (see 'What to do').

Key vocabulary: Colours of the felt pens, blotting paper, absorbs, soaks.

Organisation: Small group.

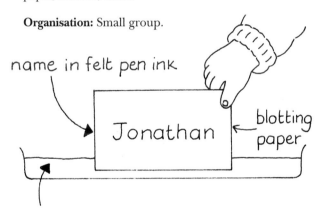

name in felt pen ink

Jonathan

blotting paper

water level must not touch ink

WHAT TO DO:

Show the group the rainbow name. What does it look like? What colours can the children see? Can children recognise any letters? Explain to the children that they are each going to make a rainbow name. Show the group how to write a name in black ink about 2 cm from the bottom of the blotting paper rectangle and to hold the paper in the water so that the ink does not touch the water (see above).

As the water is absorbed by the blotting paper it travels upwards and takes the ink with it. Black dye is made up of many colours and these separate out. As

this happens encourage children to describe what they notice. Papers should be removed from the water as soon as children are happy with their rainbow name. (**Note:** The effect will continue until the paper is dry.) Leave the names to dry on a plastic cloth.

Children may like to experiment with other colours of pens.

ACTIVITY: NOAH'S ARK

Learning opportunity: Miming animal movements.

Early Learning Goal: Physical Development. Children will be able to move with confidence, imagination and in safety.

Resources: A picture book of the story of Noah's ark.

Key vocabulary: Names of animals, words to describe movements such as hop, jump, crawl, balance, swing, stride, slow, fast, quick, long, gentle, quiet.

Organisation: Whole group in a large space.

WHAT TO DO:

Show children the pictures of the animals in the Noah story. Ask them to say how the elephant would move. Do the children think it moved quickly or slowly, quietly or noisily? What would its trunk be doing? Show children how they can be an elephant with one arm as their trunk and one as their tail. Tell the story of Noah's ark, encouraging children to mime the animals moving on board. Vary the kinds of animals to include a wide range of movements. Once all the animals are on board discuss with the children what it would have been like to be one of so many on board the ark for such a long time. How would they feel when the ark landed? Continue the story until all the animals have moved off the ark and they have seen their first rainbow.

The theme of animal movements can be extended by using benches for children to balance along.

DISPLAY

Display the animal paintings on a background of an ark which has landed beneath a large rainbow. Cover a large table with blue cloth and arrange the children's arks in the sea. Mount the rainbow names on black pieces of paper and use these to indicate who the arks belong to. Nearby put out books which tell the Noah's ark story.

BRINGING IT ALL TOGETHER

THE RAINBOW PARTY

Explain to the children that they are going to have a rainbow party. They can wear their favourite colours from the rainbow and will play rainbow games. Parents and friends will be invited to come and see their Noah's arks, join in the singing of rainbow songs and eat rainbow foods.

FOOD

Involve the children in preparing rainbow food:

- Make fruit kebabs by placing fruit pieces on cocktail sticks. Try to include as many different coloured fruits as possible. (To stop fruit pieces such as apple turning brown, rub them with lemon juice.)

- Cover rainbow shaped shortbread biscuits with white icing and multicoloured vermicelli.

- Put a teaspoon of melted chocolate in a small, sweet sized paper case with a pink or white marshmallow sweet on top. Decorate with a dab of chocolate and a Smartie to make a rainbow top hat.

RAINBOW COSTUMES

- On the day of the party invite children to come wearing articles of clothing in as many colours as possible. Some children may like to use face paint to decorate their cheeks with rainbows.

- Make triangular rainbow hats from white paper coloured with wax crayons.

RAINBOW GAMES

Before the party make a list of the group's favourite colour games which have been played during the topic. Intersperse these favourites with other, well known games which can be changed to suit the rainbow theme. Examples include:

Pass the parcel: Each wrapper is one of the colours of the rainbow.

Treasure hunt: Children go outside with an adult and try to find an object for each colour in the rainbow.

Musical rainbow: Coloured hoops are placed on the floor in an arch shape. Children walk around the room to music. When the music stops children are out if they are not standing in a hoop.

Put the counter on the rainbow: Children are blindfolded and have to place a coloured counter on a rainbow. Where the colours match they win a small prize.

After the last game seat children in a rainbow shape opposite chairs for parents and friends. Sing the rainbow songs learned in Week 6 and other colour songs sung during the term. Children might also like to recite their favourite colour finger rhymes. Finally, children can hand round the rainbow food, saving some for themselves. Invite parents to view the Noah's ark display.

RESOURCES

RESOURCES TO COLLECT

- Plant catalogues
- Paint colour charts
- Coloured acetates
- Plastic plant pots
- Pot pourri
- Pictures of road signs and colourful animals

EVERYDAY RESOURCES

- Boxes, large and small for modelling.
- Papers and cards of different weights, colours and textures, for example, sugar paper, corrugated card, silver and shiny papers, blotting paper, filter papers.
- Dry powder paints and ready-mixed paints.
- Different sized paint brushes from household brushes to thin brushes for delicate work and a variety of paint mixing containers.
- A variety of drawing and colouring pencils, crayons, pastels, charcoals, and so on.
- Additional decorative and finishing materials such as sequins, foils, glitter, tinsel, shiny wool and threads, beads, pieces of textiles, macaroni tubes and parcel ribbon.
- Table covers.
- Plastic tubs and lids from coffee jars.

STORIES

Balloon by Jez Alborough (Harper Collins).

Opposites by Nick Butterworth and Mick Inkpen (Hodder Children's Books).

The Mixed-up Chameleon by Eric Carle (Picture Puffins).

Noah's Ark by Lucy Cousins (Walker Books).

Picasso the Green Tree Frog by Amanda Graham (Era Publications).

The Blue Balloon by Mick Inkpen (Hodder Children's Books).

Mrs Jolly's Brolly by Dick King-Smith (Macdonald Young Books).

Little Red Riding Hood retold by Jonathan Langley (Collins Picture Lions).

Elmer by David McKee (Red Fox).

Elmer and the Lost Teddy by David McKee (Andersen Press).

Elmer and Wilbur by David McKee (Red Fox).

Billy's Sunflower by Nicola Moon (Little Hippo).

Winnie in Winter by Korky Paul and Valerie Thomas (Oxford University Press).

Winnie the Witch by Korky Paul and Valerie Thomas (Oxford University Press).

The Rainbow Fish by Marcus Pfister (North-South Books).

Where the Wild Things Are by Maurice Sendak (Red Fox).

POEMS

This Little Puffin by Elizabeth Matterson (Puffin).

Out and About by Shirley Hughes (Walker Books).

NON FICTION

Maisy's Colours by Lucy Cousins (Walker Books).

Colours for Katie by Richard James and Patrick Yee (Walker Books).

Eye Spy Colours by Debbie MacKinnon and Anthea Sieveking (Frances Lincoln).

Bring on the Blue by Candace Whitman (Abbeville Kids).

Ready for Red by Candace Whitman (Abbeville Kids).

Yellow and You by Candace Whitman (Abbeville Kids).

All About Colour by Irene Yates (Belitha Press).

SONGS

'Sing a Rainbow' in *Apusskido Songs for Children* chosen by Beatrice Harrop, Peggy Blakely and David Gadsby (A & C Black).

'Mr Noah Built an Ark' in *Junior Praise* compiled by Peter Horrobin and Greg Leavers (Marshall Pickering).

'Who Put the Colours in the Rainbow?' in *Come and Praise* compiled by Geoffrey Marshall-Taylor (BBC).

'Lavender's Blue' and 'Ten Green Bottles' in *Children's Birthday Songbook* arranged by Bert Brewis (International Music Publications).

'Who Built the Ark?' in *Someone's Singing Lord Hymns and Songs for Children* chosen by Beatrice Harrop (A&C Black).

COLLECTING EVIDENCE OF CHILDREN'S LEARNING

Monitoring children's development is an important task. Keeping a record of children's achievements will help you to see progress and will draw attention to those who are having difficulties for some reason. If a child needs additional professional help, such as speech therapy, your records will provide valuable evidence.

Records should be the result of collaboration between group leaders, parents and carers. Parents should be made aware of your record keeping policies when their child joins your group. Show them the type of records you are keeping and make sure they understand that they have an opportunity to contribute. As a general rule, your records should form an open document. Any parent should have access to records relating to his or her child. Take regular opportunities to talk to parents about children's progress. If you have formal discussions regarding children about whom you have particular concerns, a dated record of the main points should be kept.

KEEPING IT MANAGEABLE

Records should be helpful in informing group leaders, adult helpers and parents and always be for the benefit of the child. However, keeping records of every aspect of each child's development can become a difficult task. The sample shown will help to keep records manageable and useful. The golden rule is to keep them simple.

Observations will basically fall into three categories:

* **Spontaneous records:** Sometimes you will want to make a note of observations as they happen, for example, a child is heard counting cars accurately during a play activity, or is seen to play collaboratively for the first time.

* **Planned observations:** Sometimes you will plan to make observations of children's developing skills in their everyday activities. Using the learning opportunity identified for an activity will help you to make appropriate judgements about children's capabilities and to record them systematically.

To collect information:

* talk to children about their activities and listen to their responses;

* listen to children talking to each other;

* observe children's work such as early writing, drawings, paintings and 3D models. (Keeping photocopies or photographs is sometimes useful.)

Sometimes you may wish to set up 'one off' activities for the purposes of monitoring development. Some pre-school groups, for example, ask children to make a drawing of themselves at the beginning of each term to record their progressing skills in both co-ordination and observation. Do not attempt to make records after every activity!

* **Reflective observations:** It is useful to spend regular time reflecting on the progress of a few children (about four children each week). Aim to make some brief comments about each child every half term.

INFORMING YOUR PLANNING

Collecting evidence about children's progress is time consuming and it is important that it is useful. When you are planning, use the information you have collected to help you to decide what learning opportunities you need to provide next for children. For example, a child who has poor pencil or brush control will benefit from more play with dough or construction toys to build the strength of hand muscles.

Example of recording chart

Name: Alice Hogg		D.O.B. 26.2.97		Date of entry: 13.9.00	
Term	**Personal, Social and Emotional Development**	**Communication, Language and Literacy**	**Mathematical Development**	**Knowledge and Understanding of the World**	**Physical Development**	**Creative Development**
ONE	Reluctant to say good bye to mother. Prefers adult company 20.9.00 EMH	Enjoying listening to stories, 'Blue Balloon' a particular favourite 20.11.00 EMH	Is able to say numbers to ten and to count accurately five objects. Recognises and names squares and circles. 5.11.00 BM	Very eager to ask questions. Was fascinated by the prism. 16.10.00 AC	Can balance on one leg. Loved moving as animals and showed good imagination 16.10.00 AC	Made a wonderful newspaper collage but didn't like getting hands dirty 20.10.00 LSS
TWO						
THREE						